Teaching Proficiency T
Reading and Storytelli

This module introduces Teaching Proficiency through Reading and Storytelling (TPRS), an input-based language teaching method. TPRS provides a framework for teaching classes completely in the target language—even those at the beginner level. Through the steps of establishing meaning, creating a story that is acted out live in class, and reading, students understand and use the target language to communicate right away. Research shows that over time TPRS creates fluent speakers who excel both on traditional tests and—more importantly—in real-life situations. This is a valuable resource on TPRS for world language teachers, language teacher educators, and second language researchers.

Karen Lichtman is Assistant Professor of Spanish Linguistics and Director of Teacher Licensure in the Department of Foreign Languages and Literatures at Northern Illinois University, USA.

The Routledge E-Modules on Contemporary Language Teaching

Series Editors: Bill VanPatten, *Michigan State University, USA*, and Gregory D. Keating, *San Diego State University, USA*

The *Routledge E-Modules on Contemporary Language Teaching* series is an exciting and innovative approach to topics for the novice or in-training teacher of languages. Written in an easily accessible style and delivered in e-format and paperback versions, specialists and experts provide the latest thinking on a variety of issues that form the foundation of language-teacher knowledge and practice: the nature of language and communication, second language acquisition, interactive tasks, assessment, focus on form, vocabulary development, and technology in language teaching, among many others. Each module serves as a self-contained unit to be used on its own or as part of an introductory course on language teaching. Instructors may "mix and match" modules to create their own readings for a course on language teaching. The modules may serve as primary reading or as supplemental reading, with each module offering points of reflection, discussion questions, self-quizzes, and a reading list for those who wish to delve further into the topic.

Technology in Language Learning
An Overview
Bryan Smith

Teaching Second Language Writing
Charlene Polio

Content-Based Language Teaching
Roy Lyster

Teaching Proficiency Through Reading and Storytelling (TPRS)
An Input-Based Approach to Second Language Instruction
Karen Lichtman

For more information about this series, please visit: www.routledge.com/The-Routledge-E-Modules-on-Contemporary-Language-Teaching/book-series/REMCLT

Teaching Proficiency Through Reading and Storytelling (TPRS)

An Input-Based Approach to Second Language Instruction

Karen Lichtman

NORTHERN ILLINOIS UNIVERSITY

Routledge
Taylor & Francis Group

NEW YORK AND LONDON

First published 2018
by Routledge
711 Third Avenue, New York, NY 10017

and by Routledge
2 Park Square, Milton Park, Abingdon, Oxon, OX14 4RN

Routledge is an imprint of the Taylor & Francis Group, an informa business

© 2018 Taylor & Francis

Library of Congress Cataloging-in-Publication Data
A catalog record for this book has been requested

ISBN: 978-1-138-63281-3 (pbk)
ISBN: 978-1-315-20802-2 (ebk)

Typeset in Sabon
by Apex CoVantage, LLC

Visit the companion website to preview and purchase other modules in
this series: http://routledgetextbooks.com/textbooks/9781315679594/

Teaching Proficiency Through Reading and Storytelling (TPRS)

An Input-Based Approach to Second Language Instruction

Karen Lichtman

Overview

In this module, you will explore the following topics:

- input and comprehensible input
- input-based approaches to instruction
- Teaching Proficiency through Reading and Storytelling (TPRS)
- the principles of TPRS
- the three steps of TPRS
- TPRS skills
- techniques that complement TPRS
- current research on TPRS

Where does a baby's first word come from? Parents joyfully record that first "dada" or "no" or "uh-oh" in a baby book—but, for the baby, the celebrated first utterance is a product of a year or more of listening to language. Before babies begin to speak, they understand plenty of words and can follow commands such as "no," "touch your nose," or "look at the kitty." Children's receptive vocabulary (words they understand) is larger than their productive vocabulary (words they can say)—and this tends to last throughout life. Children learn language by pairing new words they hear with meaning, which is made clear from the context—the objects and actions in the real world that other speakers refer to. A statement like "Look! A horse!" is accompanied by clues to meaning: the presence of a real horse (or at least a horse in a picture book,) pointing, and other speakers directing their attention towards the horse. All this provides children with the meaning of the new word "horse."

Speech from parents or caregivers to children, including giving commands and naming objects in the environment, is a great example of input. **Input** is language that learners see or hear in a communicative (meaning-bearing) context. When a two-year old hears, "Don't touch that, honey. It's hot," that stretch of speech is input to the child because it is couched within the context of an adult telling the child what to do. When a Spanish student hears, "Abran los libros en la página 32" (Open your books to page 32), that stretch of speech is input to the learner because it is couched within the context of an instructor giving directions to the class. Input is indispensable in language acquisition, both first and second. Just as we must take in food in order to grow, we must take in input in order for language to grow in our heads (see, for example, the discussion in Gregory Keating's module titled *Second Language Acquisition: The Basics* in this series).

Learners must first take in input (hear new words and link them to their meaning during comprehension, process sentence structure, link grammatical forms to their meaning and functions) in order to be able to produce output (e.g., express meaning). This applies whether we are talking about a first language, or a second language. Children hear a new word such as "horse" a number of times in the context of seeing a horse, and Spanish learners hear the word "adiós" many times in the context of saying goodbye. Eventually, the child will be able to say the word "horse" to refer to a horse, and the Spanish learner will be able to say "adiós" when someone is leaving.

Of course, young children—unlike older children and adults—have thousands of hours of uninterrupted time to spend learning language. A child who hears a new language for eight hours per day at school will reach a hundred hours of language exposure in less than two weeks. In contrast, a high school student who gets three hours of language class per week will only hear the language for a little more than a hundred hours per *year*. Even if they are fortunate enough to learn in an immersion setting, older children and adults may contend with obstacles such as friends and family who want to speak to them in their native language, work, family obligations, TV, social media, and so on. The pull to use the first language is great. Given that second language learners cannot devote twenty-four hours a day, seven days a week to learning their new language, it is important that they get as much comprehensible input as possible in the very brief time they have available.

Input and Comprehensible Input

One of the major discoveries of language researchers in the 1960s and 1970s is that language acquisition is critically dependent on processing language input during communication. Whether we are talking about child first language learners or adolescent or adult second language learners, people must be engaged in communication in order to learn language. This may seem obvious regarding children, but, for some teachers, this idea seems to defy their experience with adolescents and adults. After all, don't most adolescents and adults engage in the learning of rules and vocabulary and then the practice of those items? Doesn't this lead to acquisition? The short answer is "no." Why would we say this? The Suggested Further Readings section at the end of this module provides places where the reader can explore this topic in depth, but here, we will touch briefly on two ideas. The first concerns the nature of language. The second concerns the research on attempting to teach language.

In his book *While We're On the Topic*, Bill Van Patten offers the following insight about language based on current linguistic theory and research: **Language is too abstract and complex to teach and learn explicitly.** What this claim means is that the rules and paradigms in language textbooks aren't linguistically or psycholinguistically "real." Such rules and paradigms can't reflect what actually exists in the minds of speakers of a language. On pages 24–25, Van Patten offers an example of this using the "personal *a*" in Spanish. Personal *a* is a case marker that Spanish places on the objects of prepositions when they are human, or humanlike. For instance, example (1) uses the personal *a*, but example (2) doesn't because "the material" is not human.

(1) *María conoce a Juan.* 'Mary knows John.'
(2) *María conoce la materia.* 'Mary knows the material.'

Textbooks explain this phenomenon using rules such as: In Spanish, when the direct object is a person, it is preceded by the preposition "a." This word has no English translation. The personal "a" is not used when the direct object is not a person or is an animal for which no personal feelings are felt.

This textbook rule works for the examples we saw already, but it is easy to find "exceptions" to the "rule":

(3) *Tengo una hermana.* 'I have a sister.'
(4) *El camión sigue al carro.* 'The truck is following the car.'

As we can see, "my sister" does not get the personal *a*, even though a sister is a person, and "the car" gets the personal *a*, even though a car is definitely not a person. So much for this particular rule. As Van Patten explains, the personal *a* case marker is actually controlled by "a complex interplay of abstract features such as definiteness, specificity, agency, and to a certain extent, animacy."

How do learners build such an abstract and complex linguistic system in their minds? By exposure to communicative language data (input) that is processed and "worked on" by the internal mechanisms responsible for constructing a linguistic system. The fundamental role of input in acquisition just can't be bypassed. How do we know this? From research on attempting to instruct second language learners.

The process of "teaching learners rules" is actually quite difficult. Stephen Krashen has pointed out that not even linguists—much less teachers—fully understand all the grammatical "rules" of a language. But, more importantly, even when teachers "teach rules," this does not affect the stages through which learners pass as they acquire language. As Gregory Keating explains in his module in this series, all language acquisition exhibits developmental stages and ordered development. For example, learners of English acquire —*ing* on the ends of verbs (e.g., *He's watching TV*) before they acquire past tense, —*ed* (e.g., *He watched TV*), which, in turn, is acquired before third-person, —*s*, in the present (e.g., *He watches TV*). What the research has shown is that such ordered development cannot be taught away. Even with intense practice, any effects of instruction are short-lived and ordered development soon reasserts itself. Every language teacher knows that students who have studied a language for many years can be non-nativelike on forms that were supposedly "taught" in the first week of class.

In addition to the above, there is one more reason we know input is critical for all language acquisition contexts: All advanced learners of languages have had massive exposure to language in communication. They study or live/work abroad for extended periods of time (e.g., not six weeks, but for a year or more). They marry into an L2-speaking family or environment. They watch films. They read extensively. They seek out speakers of the language. Of course, this takes time, but input and interaction with that input is the common thread in all successful cases of acquisition. What is not a common thread? Instruction in grammar. And as we noted previously, grammar instruction does little to circumvent the natural processes of acquisition.

The argument that language is acquired only by processing communicative input is complex, and we have not explored all facets of it here. However, the takeaway point is that linguists have converged on the idea that our mental representation of language does not consist of what we think of as "rules" and is not acquired through effortful study of these "rules." Instead, it is a complex and abstract system that is acquired through exposure over time to language in communicative contexts. The fundamental role of input in language acquisition is central to all current mainstream theories about second language acquisition. More specifically, the input needs to be **comprehensible input**: language that a learner can, in general, understand; language whose basic message is comprehended by the learner.

The input that helps learners develop language must be at about the right level for the learners. If we could learn from any level of input, we could pick up a new language simply by turning on the TV or the radio in that language or picking up a newspaper. This strategy wouldn't work because we wouldn't be able to understand enough of the unknown language to process it as language—rather, we would process it as mere noise. On the other hand, imagine watching a show like the educational children's TV show *Sesame Street* in an unknown language. You might be able to learn something, because some of the input from this show would be comprehensible. The show might count objects slowly while displaying numbers on the screen ("one . . . two . . . three . . . ") or repeat a phrase like "goodnight" while providing context clues, such as people going to bed or a dark sky with the moon and stars. The sentences would be shorter, the pace would be slower, words would be repeated, there would be visuals, and all these factors would help you understand the language. The more you understood, the more of the input you received would become comprehensible. Over time, this type of exposure provides the fundamental data required for building your unconscious mental representation of the language.

We mentioned earlier that comprehensible input must also have a communicative purpose: The person who speaks or writes must be trying to communicate some kind of message to the person who listens or reads. In many classrooms, this requirement is not met. Instead, a good deal of time is spent on getting learners to "practice" with language. Learners are often asked to do decontextualized activities where each sentence is not related to the next and the sentences are not communicating real meaning. For instance, learners might be asked to supply correct verb forms in sentences like "John _____ pizza. I ___ vegetables. The girls _____ dinner." We know that John and the girls are not real people, but simply subjects for example sentences. We don't really care what they (supposedly) eat. Most importantly, the purpose of these sentences is not to communicate anything but instead to practice something. And, of course, there is no input here, as no one is communicating anything to the learners, and, thus, there is nothing they need to comprehend.

Now imagine a different activity where a teacher talks about what his or her family eats for a certain holiday, like Thanksgiving. "Do you eat turkey for Thanksgiving? Yes? For Thanksgiving, my family does not eat turkey! We do not eat turkey because we are vegetarians. But we do eat mashed potatoes. I love eating mashed potatoes with vegetable gravy. Do you like mashed potatoes and gravy? We also eat green bean casserole. We eat corn and peas. We eat stuffing too, even though we do not eat turkey. My little brother only eats mashed potatoes. He is a picky eater and doesn't eat vegetables." Then, the class could compare that meal to what the students' families eat at Thanksgiving. "My family doesn't eat turkey, but does your family eat turkey? It does? My family does not eat meat, but your family eats meat. How many families eat meat for Thanksgiving? Let's make a graph. Twenty-one families eat turkey for Thanksgiving, and one family does not. Do you eat just turkey, or other meats too?" This activity has real information that is being conveyed between the teacher and students. With gestures and visual aids such as photos of food supporting the students' understanding of the message, the Thanksgiving activity would provide students with lots of comprehensible input. Learners are also engaging with the teacher in this exchange. Even though the teacher is doing most of the talking (providing input,) she asks the students questions throughout, and they provide simple answers such as "yes" and "no." This tells the teacher that they are understanding and actively processing the level-appropriate input she is providing.

Reflection

Think of a specific language class, such as the first class you took in your second language, or a class you are teaching now. What percent of class time would you say is devoted to comprehensible input? How do you know? Would this be different for a beginning language class compared to a more advanced one?

Input-Based Approaches to Instruction

Most contemporary approaches to language teaching agree that learners need lots of input. And most language teachers today would say that they are teaching "communicatively," which means that their teaching involves the communication of messages. **Communicative Language Teaching** (CLT) is a very broad term. Within the broader ideas of CLT, several **Comprehension Approaches,** or **Input-based Approaches,** can be found. Such approaches center on providing learners with as much comprehensible input as possible. Several of these are described here.

One of the earliest widespread attempts to maximize learner exposure to comprehensible input can be found in **Canadian immersion programs.** French and English are the official languages of Canada. In the 1960s and 1970s, immersion programs were developed to teach English-speaking students French. English-speaking children attended some or even all of their content courses in French. Learners were exposed to much more comprehensible input in such programs (up to six hours per day) than they would if they were in traditional language classes (only several hours per week). Because subject matter was taught in the second language, learners were actively engaged in attending to meaning (i.e., messages) in the language they were exposed to. After all, they were going to be held accountable for what they learned about history, math, and science. The teachers were bilingual and the classes provided some first language support. These programs were quite successful. Research found (perhaps not surprisingly) that the more French exposure students got (in terms of both percentage of the day taught in French and years of French), the better their French was. Students became fluent in both oral and written French. Their language production (speaking and writing) was near-native, and they were native-like when tested on their comprehension.

Because Canadian immersion students were learning the same curriculum as students who went to school in their native language (science, math, history, and so on), these programs can be seen as a form of **content-based instruction**. Content-based instruction became popular in the 1980s. Content-based classes use a second language as the medium of instruction to learn content, rather than studying language as the object of instruction. The content can be information about the cultures that speak the language, or about other school subjects. The advantages of content-based instruction are that students learn language in context, class activities tend to be more cognitively engaging, and students learn academic content. And, of course, language is used in the classroom for the communication of messages and ideas. This approach is quite popular in Europe now, where it is known as **Content and Language Integrated Learning (CLIL)**. For more information, see the module in this series by Roy Lyster called *Content-based language teaching*.

Content-based instruction was also a component of the **Natural Approach**, which was developed by Tracy Terrell in the 1970s. The Natural Approach focused on communication through talking about cultural content, talking about students' opinions, playing games, and doing problem-solving activities. This approach aims to make language learning as stress-free as possible in a communicative and input-rich environment. The teacher provides the students with large amounts of comprehensible input in the target language. The students participate only when they feel ready to speak, and they can use limited responses such as *yes/no* or other one-word answers without ever being pushed to create full sentences. Student errors are not corrected, and students never participate in language practice typical of many language classes. The Natural Approach posited that activities should be intrinsically motivating to the students. For instance, the teacher might tell a story about a cultural misunderstanding or lead the class to play a simple game such as "Go, Fish" using the target language.

The Natural Approach focused on comprehensible input and not forcing students to speak. These same principles were also key to an approach called **Total Physical Response (TPR)**, which was developed by James Asher starting in the mid-1960s. The inspiration for TPR came from watching the process of first language acquisition in young children. Asher observed that early communication with babies and toddlers often took the form of a verbal utterance by the parent followed by a physical response from the child. In a TPR lesson, the teacher gives many verbal commands to the whole class, individual students, and groups of students. The meaning of the commands is made clear through physical actions. For instance, a beginning TPR command is "stand up." The teacher will say, "stand up" in the target language, stand up himself, and perhaps gesture for the students to stand up (and expect them to do so!). Since the meaning is clear, no translation or use of the first language is needed. Hearing the language before being asked to produce it aligns with natural acquisition, and provides the data necessary for learners to begin building an unconscious mental representation of language. TPR is still used today, particularly with younger students and absolute beginners.

Reflection

None of the methods or approaches just reviewed are widespread in the United States. Why do you think this is so? Why isn't "everyone" doing some kind of input-based approach in the classroom?

Teaching Proficiency Through Reading and Storytelling (TPRS)

TPR as developed by James Asher is very effective for learning concrete vocabulary, such as physical actions and items in a classroom. However, it would be difficult to express the meaning of more abstract vocabulary, such as "democracy," "idea," or "misses someone," through a physical action. This problem was the inspiration for Teaching Proficiency through Reading and Storytelling, or TPRS. Blaine Ray, who developed TPRS, wanted to be able to teach more abstract vocabulary while retaining the benefits of TPR. Ray was a high school Spanish teacher in California. In the late 1980s, he started using TPR and elements of the Natural Approach in his classes. He found that students were very successful at the beginning of the school year, but that at some point, they would get bored with doing TPR, and he would have to resort to more traditional materials. So Ray developed what he originally called TPR Storytelling (Total Physical Response Storytelling). In 1990, he published a level 1 Spanish curriculum using his new method, titled *Look, I Can Talk*. In 1997, the first book explaining TPRS, *Fluency through TPR Storytelling: Achieving real language acquisition in school* (see Suggested Further Readings), was published by Blaine Ray and Contee Seely. This book is now in its seventh edition, with each edition containing significant changes and updates. The acronym TPRS was changed from Total Physical Response Storytelling to Teaching Proficiency through Reading and Storytelling around the year 2000, as the approach became less similar to TPR and emphasized reading more. The rest of this module will focus on TPRS, as it is one of the fastest-growing methods in language teaching in the United States today.

The Principles of TPRS

TPRS grew out of three main ideas: TPR, mastery learning (the idea that each student should get as much time and instruction as they need to understand what is being talked about), and the fundamental role of input in acquisition as explained by Stephen Krashen. In addition to step-by-step instructions for teaching using TPRS, the approach also has a well-developed set of principles. These principles allow teachers to evaluate their use of class time in terms of whether it provides the conditions under which language acquisition can occur. The following are the main principles underlying TPRS.

Students Need Huge Amounts of Input to Acquire Language

The primary goal of TPRS is to spend as much class time as possible providing students with comprehensible input through teacher speech and through reading.

Language Should Always Be Comprehensible

Although TPRS teachers speak in the target language throughout the class period, they try to ensure that every student can understand everything they say through the use of visuals, gestures, proper nouns, comprehension questions, and (when possible) cognates and glosses in the first language. Teachers who use TPRS shelter vocabulary: They either use words students already know, or else give the meaning of new words in the students' first language.

Students Should Learn a Small Number of High-Frequency Words and Phrases to Mastery

Mastery learning is an educational philosophy, popular since the late 1960s, that encourages teachers to keep teaching something in different ways until all students can achieve a certain mastery goal (for instance, 80% or 90% correct on a test of knowledge). TPRS wants students to learn the most high-frequency words in the target language to mastery. For example, the most common verbs in most languages include *to be, to have, to do, to say*, and *to go*. In TPRS, these words would be introduced in stories early in the school year, and would continue to be used very frequently by the teacher in communication until all students show that they have learned them. In contrast, early chapters of a typical textbook tend to introduce verbs that are much lower frequency in a language but center around a particular theme, such as pastimes: *to dance, to skate, to ski*, and *to paint*. If students don't learn all of these words to mastery, a traditional class may or may not move on to a new and completely different theme, such as food. Teachers who use TPRS are more likely to go "narrow and deep" with vocabulary rather than "broad and shallow."

Words Should Be Introduced in a Form in Which They Are Commonly Used

Textbooks commonly introduce verbs in the infinitive, provide full verb paradigms, and present confusing contrasts together. For example, in a traditional class with Spanish as the focus, *estar* (one of the several verbs in Spanish that means 'to be') might be presented in the infinitive (*estar*) followed by the whole paradigm (*estoy, estás, está, estamos, estáis, están*). At the same time, students might be told to use *estar* rather than *ser* (another Spanish verb meaning 'to be') for feelings (*estoy feliz* rather than *soy feliz.*) TPRS, in contrast, would introduce phrases such as *está feliz* 's/ he is happy' and *es maestra* 'she is a teacher' in stories without explaining any other person/number possibilities for the verbs or the rules about when to use which verb. TPRS understands that over time, input will provide the data that learners need to build a full mental representation, because TPRS understands the piecemeal and developmental nature of acquisition.

Class Should Be Centered Around Students and Their Interests

TPRS allows student participation in choosing topics for class discussion. Most stories feature the students themselves as main characters, and all stories are acted out by students. These topics are the most interesting to students, and students also have background knowledge about them, which helps with comprehension.

Input Must Be Structured to Ensure High Frequency for Key Items and Also Be Varied and Compelling

Frequency in the input is a key factor in acquisition. In order to learn a new word or phrase, learners need to hear and see it repeatedly. At the same time, learners must be interested in the content of the input and actively engaged in processing the meaning. So, the instructor must balance frequency (repeatedly using key items) with student interest/ engagement. Later, we will see how this is done in TPRS.

Students Work on Comprehension Before Working on Production

The idea behind this principle is that students should never be forced to produce language. Once the students begin to build a mental representation of language they can tap for self-expression, they will voluntarily produce language. Another way to state this is that learner production of language is allowed to emerge on its own. Thus, TPRS focuses on student comprehension (listening and reading) rather than production (speaking and writing).

Only Minimal Class Time Should Be Used for Learner Output

This principle follows from the previous one. Because language is best acquired when students' internal learning mechanisms are processing comprehensible input, student output (students speaking and writing the language) should occupy only a few minutes of each class period. The most important function of student output is to let the teacher know where students are in terms of their language acquisition. If the teacher notices students having difficulty with something in particular, the teacher will work to include more examples of it in the input.

Reflection

The principles just reviewed are specific to TPRS. However, do you see them as useful for other kinds of instructional formats and approaches? What additional principles for language teaching do you think are important?

The Three Steps of TPRS

TPRS outlines a series of three steps to organize class time: (1) establish meaning, (2) ask a story, and (3) reading.

Establish Meaning

The purpose of the first phase of a TPRS lesson is to get students familiar with words and phrases used during the subsequent phases. In this phase, the teacher begins by introducing a set of new target language words and structures to the students using gestures, visuals, and/or glosses in the first language to clearly establish their meaning. "Structures" has a special meaning to the TPRS community—probably closest to what the average person thinks of as "words and phrases." For instance, *una bebida* 'a drink' is one structure, and *quería ir* '(someone) wanted to go' would be another structure. Often, three structures are introduced each day of class.

There is no grammar teaching, as in traditional classrooms. Instead, pieces and parts of grammatical structures are introduced as parts of words or phrases. Thus, the teacher does not introduce "the present tense" in Spanish, for example. Instead, the teacher introduces the phrase *baila mucho* 's/he dances a lot.' This is because the story being created is in the present and about a single character. The teacher might also ask other students in the class *¿Bailas mucho?* 'Do you dance a lot?' in order to compare them to the main character. In this way, the students have been exposed to two different present tense verb forms, but only when they are naturally required for communication. In general, for languages that have different person and number endings on verbs, the third-person singular tends to be the first form introduced in TPRS. A simple Google search will show that the third-person singular also tends to be the highest-frequency verb form in natural language use: *está* 's/he is' is currently used on the internet five times more frequently than *estoy* 'I am.'

If the new phrases can be communicated through gestures or actions, they are usually introduced by saying the word in the target language while doing the action. However, it is still desirable to explicitly give the meaning of the words at some point in order to avoid misunderstandings like the difference between "goes" and "walks," which could be difficult to make clear using only gestures. If the new phrases can be communicated using pictures or visuals, they will be introduced by saying the target language word while pointing to or otherwise interacting with the visual. More abstract or complex words will usually be written on the board in the target language together with their meaning in the students' native language (obviously, this will be impossible when the students speak many first languages—perhaps, in that case, each student could look the word up in his/her bilingual dictionary instead). Regardless of concreteness versus abstractness of words and how they are introduced, it is key in TPRS that teachers use the structures many times in their input as part of the lesson. Students may not be comfortable producing a structure to communicate meaning until after they have heard the teacher use it in communication ten, twenty, or thirty times or more. (See the earlier principle about the role of output in the TPRS classroom.)

How do teachers achieve so many uses of the new phrases? They may give the class commands in the style of Total Physical Response. If the new structure is *quería bailar* 'wanted to dance,' the teacher's narrative might be something like this (in the target language, of course): "Wanted to dance. [teacher acts out 'wanted' with hands clasped together, followed by 'dance'; students copy this action] Wanted to dance. [everyone acts out wanted to dance again] Class, wanted to dance. [students do the actions again] John, wanted to dance. [just John does the actions] Sarah, wanted to dance. [just Sarah does the actions] Everybody, wanted to dance. [the whole class does the actions]."

The new structure is combined with previously learned words, cognates, and proper nouns to keep the language comprehensible. This enables constructions like: "Girls, wanted to dance. [just the girls do the actions] Boys, wanted to dance. [just the boys do the actions] Wanted to dance slowly. [everyone does the actions slowly] Wanted to dance fast. [everyone does the actions quickly] Wanted to dance in a circle. [everyone does the actions while moving in a circle or turning around] Wanted to dance the Macarena. [everyone gestures "wanted" and then tries to do the movements of the Macarena. Note that it doesn't matter how accurately the Macarena is represented, for instance, just whether the students have understood the command and are trying to carry it out.] Wanted to dance salsa. [everyone gestures "wanted" and tries to dance salsa] Wanted to dance like Michael Jackson. [everyone gestures "wanted" and tries to dance like Michael Jackson] Wanted to dance like Justin Bieber. [everyone gestures "wanted" and tries to dance like Justin Bieber] Wanted to dance with a friend. [everyone gestures "wanted" and pretends to dance with another student]."

At this point, the teacher has said, 'wanted to dance' sixteen times, but none of these utterances have really been in natural contexts. Next, the teacher will often personalize the vocabulary by asking the students questions about themselves: "Class, who wanted to dance on Friday? [some students raise hands] Who wanted to dance on Saturday? [some students raise hands, someone calls out "Sarah"] Sarah, you wanted to dance? [Sarah: yes] Did you want to dance on Friday, or Saturday? [Sarah: Saturday] Class, Sarah wanted to dance on Saturday. [class: ohhh] Sarah, where did you want to dance on Saturday? [Sarah does not reply] Did you want to dance in school? [Sarah: no] Did you want to dance in Wal-Mart? [Sarah: no] Did you want to dance in Mexico? [Sarah: house] Oh, you wanted to dance in your house? [Sarah: yes] Class, Sarah wanted to dance in her house on Friday. [class: ohhh] Did you want to dance alone, or did you want to dance with someone? [class: with someone] Did you want to dance with someone famous? [class: yes] Class, which famous person did Sarah want to dance with? [class says various famous people's names] Did she want to dance with Donald Trump?" This type of interaction is called Personalized Questions and Answers and abbreviated PQA.

At this point, 'wanted to dance' has been said over thirty times and has been used for **communication** in **different, meaningful contexts**. By **communication**, we mean that previously unknown information is being exchanged. The teacher did not know that Sarah wanted to dance, or where she wanted to dance. Even if some of the "information" in TPRS is made up (we don't know whether Sarah really wanted to dance, or if a friend is just putting her forward as a story character), this type of information exchange is very different from a display context where students are only expected to produce one specific correct answer that the teacher already knows (e.g., when a teacher asks "What color is a banana?" **Different** contexts mean that the structure is used in different sentences, not over and over again in the same sentence. For instance, a German teacher could ask "Magst du Pizza?" and "Magst du Coke?" to use "do you like" in two different contexts. **Meaningful** contexts mean that the structure must be used to communicate with students. In the "do you like" example, the teacher really does not know whether each student likes pizza or

Coke, so information is being exchanged. Thus, even though each word is used repeatedly, because this use is in different, meaningful contexts, TPRS is very different from a non-meaningful "listen-and-repeat" activity.

If three structures were introduced, they would be mixed together during this part of the lesson (rather than using one thirty times before moving on to the next), which adds more variation and interest as meaning is established. For instance, if the structures were *quería bailar* 'wanted to dance,' *fue* 'went,' and *vio* 'saw,' the original TPR might sound like, "Wanted to dance. [students do the actions] Saw. [students do an action for "saw," such as pointing at their eyes and then at an object] Wanted to dance. [students do the actions] Jenny, wanted to dance. [Jenny does the actions] Went. [students gesture using a pointing finger moving in a particular direction] Boys, went. [the boys do the action] Girls, went quickly. [the girls do the action] Everyone, saw quickly. [students do the action for "saw" quickly] Wanted to dance slowly. [students do the actions slowly]." The new phrases would also be mixed together as the teacher started asking students questions about their own interests.

Ask a Story

In the second phase of the lesson, the teacher and the students co-construct a story. The co-construction of a story by the teacher and students together is the central, distinctive feature of TPRS. The goal of the story-asking step is to create a shared context for communication between the students and teacher (the story.) A byproduct of this is that story-asking provides students with repeated exposure to new language structures using engaging and varied comprehensible input.

This step is called "Ask a story" rather than "Tell a story" because the teacher is not telling a pre-made story with all details and plot points already determined. Instead, the teacher has some basic story elements in mind and spends the class time asking students questions and incorporating student answers into the story. Thus, the story will be different with each group of students. The teacher's rough outline of the story is prepared before class. Here is a sample story outline that a beginning TPRS teacher might use: A character wanted to dance but went to a location where she could not dance, and then, finally, she went to a location where she could dance. This example is typical of TPRS story outlines:

- the story involves a problem;
- the story goes to more than one location to solve the problem;
- and the story has an eventual solution.

Many details still need to be filled in, though, such as the character's name, why she wanted to dance (and/or where, with whom), why she couldn't dance in the first location, what the second location is, how she arrived at the second location, and so on.

As the teacher sets up and guides the story, the students are invited to suggest details. The teacher entertains several suggestions before picking one to be the official story detail (or, instead, selecting a new detail that was not suggested by students.) For instance, part of the teacher's questioning might look like this: "What was the girl's name? [Students provide several suggestions.] Was the girl named María, or Elena? [Some students: María. Other students: Elena.] Yes, of course, the girl was named María Elena."

Students are expected to answer questions using previously learned vocabulary, proper names, and cognates, rather than the new structures of the day. This fits with the TPRS principle to maximize input and not force student output. Beginning classes might answer mostly *yes/no* or *either/or* questions, but they can also answer more complex questions if the teacher phrases them carefully. For instance, lower-level students might respond to "Why was the girl named María Elena?" with a one-word answer such as "mamá," indicating that her mother chose the name. The teacher could build on this response by restating it as a full sentence. Alternatively, the teacher might ask the question and provide some options for students to select from, scaffolding their answers. For instance, "Why was the girl named María Elena? (1) Because that was her mother's name, or (2) Because that was her grandmother's name?" In an upper-level class, the teacher might just ask the question and wait to see if students are able to give their own full-sentence responses. "Why" questions require the most difficult answers in terms of the demands for students to produced language, but they can be tailored to the students' level and provide opportunities for critical thinking.

As the story unfolds, it is acted out by the students, with constant direction from the teacher. The teacher tells the "actors" where to stand and what to do, either "secretly" by whispering in the first language, or in the target language. For instance, when a new location is selected based on student suggestions, the teacher would direct the actor to walk to that location as represented by a certain place in the classroom. Teachers may also provide characters with lines of dialogue which they incorporate into the scene they are enacting. The talk between the teacher and student actors provides more opportunities to use the target structures and also allows more use of first- and second-person verb forms.

Story-asking provides students with lots of level-appropriate input. The repetitive questioning techniques (see the later section on Circling) serve as constant comprehension checks, and the presence of live actors creates a shared context that also boosts comprehension. The opportunity for students to suggest story details increases engagement and provides opportunities for real communication, since the teacher does not know what the students will suggest, and the students do not know what will happen in the story. Note that the live co-construction of the story makes this type of story-acting very different from the skits and "dialogues" that students are often asked to perform in a traditional classroom. Skits and "dialogues" use a pre-written script. The process of the teacher and students agreeing on what will happen next in the story is where the real communication occurs in TPRS.

TPRS stories can be very simple. A typical one would be "A boy wanted a dog. He went to France to look for dogs, but there were no dogs there, only cats. So, the boy went to Belgium. In Belgium there were dogs, but they were too expensive. Finally, the boy went to Switzerland. In Switzerland the dogs were all free, so the boy took seven dogs home. He was very happy and the dogs were happy too." This story would provide many contexts for use of words and phrases including "dog," "he went," "there were," and "wanted," among others.

After the story is "asked," a number of activities are possible. A few examples are given later. To review the story and get more input, the students may be asked to do activities such as:

- listen to the teacher retell the story;
- listen to the teacher retell the story while intentionally making factual errors (the students will correct those errors);
- act out the story in groups as the teacher retells it (if there were three actors in the story, the class gets into groups of three, and each student takes a role);
- draw the story in the style of a comic strip as the teacher retells it;
- listen to the teacher read statements from the story out of order and match those statements to pictures.

Students may also be invited to produce some output at this point so that the teacher can check student progress. If students have difficulty doing any of these activities, then this serves as feedback to the teacher that more input is required! Students may be asked to:

- retell the story orally to a classmate or in a small group;
- retell the story while acting it out with a partner or in a group;
- write down the story (within a time limit or at a more leisurely pace);
- write captions for pictures of the story;
- write a different ending for the story.

Finally, output and input can be combined in activities such as retelling the story as a class while the teacher writes it on the board or types it using a computer projected on a large screen for students to see. In this case, students produce output when they contribute information to the story and receive input as they read what the teacher is writing.

Reading

In the "reading" phase of a lesson, the students transition from processing aural input to processing written input. The goals of the reading step are to provide additional comprehensible input and acquaint students with the written word. Thus, the reading materials will have been selected or created to include a very high proportion of known vocabulary (along with cognates and proper nouns) so that students will easily understand the text without needing to use glosses or a dictionary.

The written input is often related to the new words and phrases of the day; it may be a version of the class story written ahead of time by the teacher. Another reading option is a set of scaffolded readings called "embedded reading," which is described later in the section about reading materials. At other times, the reading material is a text that is comprehensible but not tied to the new words and phrases that the class is learning, such as a novella written for learners or free voluntary reading of children's books in the target language. This type of reading simply provides more comprehensible input, without that input being targeted to the new words and phrases that the class is learning.

Of course, understanding reading is much easier when the students' native language and the target language share the same writing system. When this is not the case, a technique called Cold Character Reading is effective for facilitating early literacy in Chinese, Japanese, and other languages with non-Roman writing systems. Cold Character Reading presents students with text in the target language (and the target writing system) which is exclusively made up of language they have already learned orally. The teacher leads students in slowly reading the text out loud as a group. Students are soon able to read never-before-seen characters for words they have learned, as they use context to predict which words will probably come next. For more information on Cold Character Reading, consult Terry Waltz's book *TPRS with Chinese Characteristics*.

Many discussion techniques are used to make sure students are engaged in reading and fully comprehending the written text. Students may be asked to answer questions about the story, retell the story to a classmate, draw pictures of the story, rewrite the story, spot differences between the class's created story and the written version of the story, tell how they would have responded to the situation in the story, add additional details to the story, or write a new ending for the story. An additional option for checking reading comprehension is translation. If the students' first language is English, the teacher will have them read the story (which is written in the target language) out loud in English, either individually or as a whole class. That is, while students look at a text saying, "María quería bailar con . . .," what they say out loud is "Maria wanted to dance with . . . "

These discussion techniques are appropriate when the students are all reading the same text. Another way TPRS includes written input is to let each student choose their own texts to read silently in the target language.

This is called "free voluntary reading." Research on the benefits of free voluntary reading shows that it helps learners build both vocabulary and productive language skills, such as speaking and writing. It also allows students to select easier or more difficult texts based on their personal levels of reading comprehension, providing an opportunity for differentiation. The later section on developing or finding comprehensible reading materials gives ideas for developing a classroom library suitable for free voluntary reading.

Throughout the three steps of TPRS, teachers avoid forcing students to speak (students volunteer to participate in helping to construct the story by adding details), explicitly correcting errors, teaching grammar or rules, and letting vocabulary go "out-of-bounds" by saying something the students do not understand. Instead, they focus on providing comprehensible input, both orally and through reading.

Quiz

Take the following short quiz to see what you have learned so far. The answers are provided at the end.

1. Which of the following is NOT a principle of TPRS?

    a. Class should be completely comprehensible to students.
    b. Student interests should determine class topics.
    c. Groups of related vocabulary words should be learned together (i.e. foods, clothing items, colors.)

2. According to TPRS principles, which activity is the best use of class time?

    a. students writing
    b. students listening
    c. students speaking

3. Appropriate readings for a TPRS class are those that . . .

    a. deal with real-world situations.
    b. contain mostly known vocabulary.
    c. are written by members of the target cultures, for members of the target cultures.

4. Which is true of the Establish Meaning step?

    a. Translation should be avoided.
    b. Verbs should be introduced in the infinitive form.

    c. Gestures should be used to introduce and work with the new structures.

5. During the Ask a Story step, students . . .

    a. try to guess what the teacher's pre-planned story is.
    b. can suggest details that will be incorporated into the story.
    c. are expected to write down the story as it is told.

6. Which of these is part of TPRS but NOT part of TPR?

    a. Student actors act out a story.
    b. The teacher gives the students commands.
    c. New words and phrases are repeated many times.

[Answers. 1. c; 2. b; 3. b; 4. c; 5. b; 6. a]

TPRS Skills

TPRS can look very easy if you are observing an experienced teacher. However, experienced TPRS teachers are actually simultaneously using many skills that they have developed through work and reflection over time. A number of these skills are detailed here: lesson and unit planning, comprehension checks, circling (repetitive questioning), pop-up grammar, developing or finding comprehensible reading materials, adapting a textbook, assessment, and miscellaneous skills.

Lesson and Unit Planning

How does a teacher plan a TPRS lesson (one day's activities) or unit (group of several days' class activities)? The three steps (establishing meaning, asking a story, and reading) do not all necessarily take place during the same class period. In fact, *Fluency Through TPR Storytelling* suggests that a five-day week use Monday and Tuesday to establish meaning and ask a story (the story from Monday carrying over into Tuesday), Wednesday and Thursday to read and discuss an extended reading based on the class story, and Friday to assess and read an unrelated reading, such as a novella. Experienced TPRS teachers are able to "slow down" stories so that a single story lasts several days using this variety of activities. Experienced teachers also tend to be more fluid with how they use class time, cutting off a story that is not interesting or expanding on a story that is highly engaging.

    One way to plan a unit is around a "chapter story," which is simply a longer story. TPRS curricula often have chapter stories with about twelve or fifteen structures. The structures are divided into groups of three that can be introduced on a given class day (depending on the pace of the class). When the class is ready for the chapter story, they will have already learned all the new structures. Here is an example based on the classic story of the *Three Little Pigs*.

Chapter story: Three little pigs built houses. The first little pig did not work hard and built a house out of straw. The second little pig worked hard and built a house out of sticks. The third little pig worked very hard for three days and built a house out of bricks.

The next day, a wolf came. He knocked on the door of the straw house and shouted, "Little pig, little pig, let me in!" The pig shouted, "No!" The wolf said, "Then I'll blow your house down!" He blew the house down, but the pig ran away and hid in the house of sticks.

The wolf said, "Little pigs, little pigs, let me in!" The pigs shouted, "No!" The wolf said, "Then I'll blow your house down!" He blew the house down, but the pigs ran away and hid in the house of bricks.

The wolf shouted, "Little pigs, little pigs, let me in!" The pigs shouted, "No!" The wolf said, "Then I'll blow your house down!" But the wolf could not blow the house down. The wolf went down the chimney to eat the pigs, but the pigs caught him and ate him for dinner.

Choosing the important, non-cognate structures from this story that the students don't already know might yield the following structures:

---

three little pigs	built a house	worked very hard	straw	sticks
bricks	wolf	knocked on the door	shouted	let me in
ran away	hid in	went down the chimney	eat/ate	caught

These words might be broken up into five stories. Here is an idea of which words and phrases could be featured in each story and a possible story idea (in parentheses) with which to use them.

Days 1–2: worked very hard, hid in, wolf (One wolf worked very hard, while another wolf hid in his bedroom and didn't work). The three steps of TPRS (establish meaning, ask a story, read) would all take place with this "mini-story" and each "mini-story" that follows, including the chapter story.

Days 3–4: built a house, bricks, went down the chimney (Someone built a house out of bricks so Santa could go down the chimney on Christmas Eve).

Days 5–6: shouted, straw, eat/ate (A goat keeps eating all the straw, and the farmer shouts at it).

Days 7–8: knocked on the door, stick, let me in (Someone knocks on a door with a stick and asks to be let in, but the person inside won't let them in).

Days 9–10: ran away, three little pigs, caught (Three little pigs ran away from their mother, and their mother caught them one by one).

Days 11–13: Chapter story.

As you might infer, days 1–10 described earlier use regular TPRS lessons to "prep" students for the chapter story they will read on days 11–13. Prior to the chapter story, students do not need to know that they will be reading about three little pigs and what happened to them. They are not getting "snippets" of the final story as part of the prep. Instead, days 1–10 use different storylines to make the words and phrases familiar so that the chapter story's content is maximally comprehensible on days 11–13.

Comprehension Checks

The goal of TPRS teachers is to be maximally comprehensible. They want *everything* they say to be comprehensible, to *everyone*, including those students who lag behind their peers in comprehension ability. This ensures that no students get lost or tune out the teacher's input because they do not understand. For this reason, teachers use frequent **comprehension checks** during each lesson. These checks may take place during all of the three steps. There are many techniques for checking students' comprehension:

- Teachers often ask students to hold up their fingers according to how well they are understanding the lesson. Ten fingers indicate perfect comprehension, whereas one finger indicates very low comprehension. Based on student responses, the teacher will adjust the pace of his or her speech and instruction until the whole class indicates that they comprehend all or nearly all of the lesson.
- If and when students have the same first language, direct translation to the students' first language is useful as a fast comprehension check. Teachers may ask for translations of single words, whole sentences, or the teacher's questions. For instance, a German teacher may ask, "What does *ging* mean?", expecting students to say "went." (Now any students who forgot the word *ging* have been reminded of its meaning as well.) To check a whole sentence from the story, the teacher would say the sentence, "Der Junge ging in den Laden" and then ask, "What did I say?" This checks whether students are able to

interpret the sentence as "The boy went to the store." If the teacher asks a question such as "Wohin ging der Junge?" and the class does not answer it immediately, the teacher might say, "Wohin ging der Junge—what did I ask?" If the class is able to state the meaning of the question as "To where did the boy go" or "Where did the boy go to," the teacher knows they understand the question, and they will also be more ready to answer the question. Translation is a brief break in a class otherwise conducted in the target language, but it can provide an efficient and unambiguous comprehension check.

- Teachers look for very quick, automatic answers to their repetitive questions, described in the next section. The teacher peppers the class with *yes/no*, *either/or*, and *wh*-questions. When these questions are about known information from the story, nearly all of the students should be able to answer them quickly. This shows that they are processing the language at a natural speed.

- Another technique for gauging comprehension is the use of "exit tickets." An exit ticket is a small slip of paper that students turn in at the end of class, responding to a prompt from the teacher. Exit tickets provide the teacher with quick, anonymous feedback about the class. For example, the teacher might ask what percent of the class students understood, what were some new words they learned that day, or what part of the story was hardest to understand. Other teachers ask more complex, higher order thinking questions on exit tickets. The teacher would then read the exit tickets and use that information to adjust the next day's lesson plan.

Circling

A staple of TPRS is **circling**. Circling is simply asking repetitive questions about the same detail of a story. Circling serves to build students' ability to process and respond to questions, check student comprehension, provide additional uses of the new language structures, and keep students engaged. Here is a typical example of circling (try to imagine how this would be done in the language you teach).

- The teacher says a statement: "Donald wanted to be president." (Students are typically coached to react to statements with a response such as "Ohhh.")
- *Yes/no* question about the statement: "Did Donald want to be president? Yes, or no?" (Students: "Yes.")
- *Either/or* question: Did Donald want to be president, or did he want to play baseball? (Students: "President.")
- *Yes/no* question with a negative answer: "Did Donald want to play baseball?" (Students: "No.")

- Restate the negative and restate the positive: "Right, Donald did not want to play baseball; he wanted to be president." (Students: "Ohhh.")
- *wh*-question about the original statement: "What country did Donald want to be president of?" (Students: "The United States!" "Mexico!" "Russia!")
- Original statement with new detail: "Yes, Donald wanted to be president of Russia." (Students: "Ohhh.")

Reflection

Review the teacher's use of circling in the previous example. How do you think the teacher keeps the questioning interesting? How would the teacher use body language, facial gestures, and other aspects of non-verbal communication to engage students? How would you keep it interesting if you were circling in your target language?

While the example of circling you just read is typical, the teacher cannot simply repeat the questions in the same order every time. If so, students will learn to anticipate the answers. Questions should be asked in different orders. Here is an example of a similar script in a more random order:

- Statement: "Donald wanted to be president." (Students: "Ohhh.")
- *Yes/no* question: "Did Donald want to be president of Mexico? Yes, or no?" (Students: "No.")
- *Yes/no* question: "Did Donald want to be president?" (Students: "Yes.")
- Restate the statement with the new detail: "Right, Donald wanted to be president, but he did not want to be president of Mexico." (Students: "Ohhh.")
- *wh*-question: "What country did Donald want to be president of?" (Students: "The United States!" "Spain!" "Russia!")
- *Either/or question*: "Did Donald want to be president of the United States, or of Russia?" (Students: "Russia!")
- Restate the statement with the new detail: "Yes, Donald wanted to be president of Russia." (Students: "Ohhh.")

Questions can be asked about any part of the sentence, including the subject of the sentence, the verb or action, or details contained in something like a prepositional phrase. Let's take the sample sentence "Christopher Columbus sailed to America." The teacher might circle (ask questions about) the subject (Who sailed to America? Did Christopher Columbus or Christopher Robin sail to America?). The verb could be the focus of questions (Did Columbus sail to America, or did he swim to America? Did he sail to America quickly, or slowly?). And, the teacher could also circle information contained in the prepositional phrase (Did he sail to America or to India? Did he sail to America or around America?).

Different types of questions can be ranked according to their difficulty—based on what the learner needs to *produce* in order to answer the question. If students do not respond quickly to a question, it is usually a sign that they either do not understand the question or do not have enough language to answer the question. The teacher will ask an easier question to make sure the students understand, and then return to the more difficult question, possibly with extra support such as suggesting possible answers to the students. From easiest to hardest, the types of questions are:

- *Yes/no* questions
- *Either/or* questions
- *wh*-questions (who, what, when, where) that require a one-word answer
- *wh*-questions that require a longer answer (such as why and how)

The easier questions used during circling are display questions: questions that the teacher already knows the answer to, which are really prompts for students to display their knowledge or comprehension. Display questions are not used much in everyday life outside the classroom. A classic example of a display question is "What color is a banana?" (It's yellow.) However, every time the teacher asks for student suggestions in TPRS, the teacher does not know in advance what the suggestions will be. And every time the teacher adds a new piece of information to the plot of the story, the students do not know in advance where the story will go. In any case, all the questions—display questions and real questions—keep students engaged and provide additional uses of the new language structures in varied contexts.

The circling technique is not limited to use during storytelling: It can also be used while discussing a reading and even when having conversations with students about their own lives.

Pop-Up Grammar

Even though an underlying premise of acquisition is that language is abstract and complex and can't be learned in traditional ways, almost all teachers occasionally feel the need to teach or at least point out some "grammar" points. TPRS accepts this impulse but tries to limit the amount of class time spent on it using a technique called **pop-up grammar**. The term "pop-up grammar" comes from a TV show called *Pop-Up Video*. This show played music videos while text bubbles containing trivia or jokes about the video appeared briefly on the screen. Pop-up grammar consists of five-second grammar explanations that the teacher makes, usually while discussing a reading (see the third step of TPRS described previously). These explanations are given in the students' first language when possible, so that all students understand them. According to the guidelines of ACTFL, the American Council on the Teaching of Foreign Languages, 90% of the class should be conducted in the target language. TPRS considers pop-up grammar to be a good use of the 10% of the class in which students and teachers can use the first language. (Teachers of students with a variety of L1s could try explaining in the target language using words that the students already know, such as "Girl: one girl. GirlS: two girls.")

To see an example of a pop-up grammar explanation for Spanish, consider the sentence *Me gustan las verduras* ('I like vegetables,' or 'Vegetables are pleasing to me.') A traditional grammar explanation might say that the verb *gustar* has the third-person plural ending—*n* because 'vegetables' is a plural noun. An example of a TPRS teacher's pop-up grammar explanation would be "See the—*n* on *gustan*? The—n is there because there are many vegetableS that please me, not just one vegetable." On a later exposure, the teacher could ask, "Why does it say *Me gustan las verduras* and not *Me gusta las verduras*? Right, the—*n* goes on the end of *gusta* because more than one kind of vegetable pleases me." Pop-up grammar explanations avoid the use of metalinguistic terminology (i.e., technical terms used to refer to language like *split infinitive* or *verb inflection*) and instead focus on the meaning of the grammar points. Grammar is highlighted only to show how it relates to the meaning of a message.

To give an example of a brief "grammar explanation" from another language, a French teacher might say, "Why is 'a handsome boy' *un beau garçon* and not *un garçon beau*? Right, if we are talking about physical appearance, then we put *handsome* before *boy*." After this explanation, the teacher will immediately return to discussing the events in the story using the target language.

Developing or Finding Comprehensible Reading Materials

Because of its focus on keeping class completely comprehensible—together with the use of lots of written input—TPRS demands a different approach to finding or creating reading materials than other teaching methods. Most textbooks try to include "authentic" readings (texts created by the target cultures, for an audience of readers from the target cultures), but because authentic materials often have high vocabulary and grammar demands, textbooks provide glosses of words and grammar items they don't expect the students to know. TPRS sees little value in this because if the word is simply mentioned once in a reading and glossed, students are not likely to acquire it. Remember what we said about the need to ensure high frequency of key items in the input earlier in the module.

If reading materials are to be completely comprehensible and tailored to each class's level, they must usually be created by teachers or other authors who understand the nature of acquisition and the importance of comprehensibility. The simplest source of inspiration for reading materials is the stories created in class. For example, the French teacher who was introducing the phrase "a handsome boy" could write a story about a handsome boy. The teacher who was asking about Donald wanting to be president could write a story about a student who wanted to be president of his class.

However, reading materials can be about anything, so long as they are comprehensible. Teachers can write nonfiction about current events, school events, their own lives, and students' lives. Many teachers get inspiration for stories from cultural folktales, legends, and movies. Teachers have also published commercially available mini-stories, such as the *Cuéntame/Raconte-Moi* ('Tell Me') curriculum series by Christine Anderson, Valerie Marsh, Carol Gaab, Kristy Placido, and others. There is also the *Look, I Can Talk!* series by Blaine Ray and others.

Novellas written for language learners are also a major source of reading material. The first such book, Blaine Ray's *Pobre Ana*, created a 6,000-word story at the novice mid level using a vocabulary of only 300 different words. The story deals with a girl from California who is jealous of richer friends. After she travels to Mexico and sees the level of poverty there, she becomes more thankful for what she has. Many of the novellas deal with similar themes of American children who travel to other countries, but newer books also include people from the target cultures as main characters. These books are available in Spanish, French, German, Chinese, and English, among other languages.

Newer novellas such as Carol Gaab's *Brandon Brown dice la verdad* ('Brandon Brown Tells the Truth') have been written using as few as seventy-five unique vocabulary words, plus cognates with English, to create a story that is 4,100 words long. This book provides repeated exposure to fifteen core verbs including *decir* 'to say,' which is used ninety-five times, *estar* 'to be,' which is used seventy-six times, and *escuchar* 'to hear/listen,' which is used fifty-eight times. Books are available in multiple genres, including humor (*Brandon Brown* series; also available in six other languages), narrative nonfiction (*Esperanza; Felipe Alou*), culture-based suspense, mystery, or adventure (*La maldición de la cabeza reducida* 'The Mystery of the Shrunken Head'/*Problèmes au Paradis* 'Problems in Paradise'), adventure (*Piratas del Caribe y el mapa secreto* 'Pirates of the Caribbean and the Secret Map'/*Pirates français des Caraïbes* 'French Pirates of the Caribbean'), supernatural or sci-fi fiction (*Noches misteriosas en Granada/Nuits mystérieuses à Lyon* 'Mysterious Nights in Granada/Lyon'), environmental fiction (*Robo en la noche* 'Robbery in the Night'/*Le Vol des oiseaux* 'The Flight of the Birds'), historical fiction (*Rebeldes de Tejas* 'Rebels from Texas'), modernized legend (*La Llorona de Mazatlán* 'The Weeping Woman from Mazatlán'), magical realism (*Vector*), and more.

Children's books, especially those with limited text and lots of illustrations, are another good source of authentic, comprehensible, reading material. Teachers find children's books in the language section of bookstores, at conferences, and on trips to countries where the target language is spoken. Spanish teachers in the United States also have domestic options for children's books, such as Scholastic book orders.

Many teachers consider students to be ready to read a book on their own when they know 90% of the vocabulary. (This can be determined by asking the students to count the number of words they do not know out of the first 100 words of the book. If the students count ten or fewer unknown words, then they have the ability to understand the book on their own.) If the teacher directs the reading as a whole-class activity, the books can be a little less comprehensible—but students should still know 75% of the vocabulary words to be ready for a reading. However, these guidelines are suggestions and have not been tested through actual research on reading comprehension. In fact, Paul Nation's research on reading in a second language (see Suggested Further Readings) recommends much higher levels of vocabulary knowledge—98% of words should be known for students to read a fiction text on their own! Regardless of the exact percentages, the takeaway message here is that in order for a text to support language acquisition, it should be engaging and mostly comprehensible to students.

Reflection

Think about when you first began to read something "serious" in your second language. Was this in a class? How easy or difficult was the experience? What do you have difficulty reading in your second language now, if anything? Can you read without a dictionary handy? Now try to imagine the first year student of your language. What kind of text can that person realistically handle without difficulty?

If teachers want to work with more difficult or authentic texts, one way to build up student skills is to begin with a very basic version of a text, work up to an intermediate version, and finally tackle the advanced or authentic text. This technique, developed by Laurie Clarcq and Michele Whaley, is known as **embedded reading**. (The term *embedded reading* is not completely transparent, but is meant to refer to the idea that the basic version of the reading is "embedded" or contained in each of the more difficult versions of the text, as you will see) This scaffolding technique builds students' confidence, schema for the reading, and vocabulary so that they can eventually handle the original authentic text. Here is a brief example of embedded reading in Spanish and in English, taken from the first pages of a Spanish children's book called *Esteban y el escarabajo* ('Esteban and the scarab beetle').

> *Una tarde, Esteban descubrió un escarabajo. Casi sin pensarlo, se quita un zapato y lo empuña en el aire como un arma.*

> 'One afternoon, Esteban discovered a scarab beetle. Almost without thinking, he takes off a shoe and holds it in the air like a weapon.'

These sentences have a lot of difficult vocabulary words, but they don't actually convey much information. More simplified versions would be:

> *Esteban descubrió un insecto. Sin pensar, se quita un zapato y lo tiene en la mano.*

> 'Esteban discovered an insect. Without thinking, he takes off a shoe and has it in his hand.'

By using the cognate "insect" and removing nuances such as "one afternoon" and "almost," these sentences are easier to understand. But the sentences can be even simpler:

> *Esteban ve un insecto. Pone un zapato en la mano.*

> 'Esteban sees an insect. He puts a shoe in his hand.'

This version has only the critical information in the text. Students would first read the most simplified version. When they understand it, they would be ready for the medium-difficulty version and, finally, the original, authentic text. The information they gain at each stage of the reading makes it easier to understand and acquire words from context while reading the next most difficult version.

Embedded readings can be created from the "top down," as in the example from *Esteban y el escarabajo*, by deleting about 1/4 of the text for each simpler version. They can also be created from the "bottom up" by starting with some simple sentences and adding new information, such as connecting words, details, and dialogue.

Adapting a Textbook

Commercially available textbooks are based on principles that are very different from the principles of TPRS described in this module. Typical textbooks contain vocabulary lists, explicit grammar explanations and practice, and few activities devoted to actual communication (the expression, interpretation, and negotiation of meaning in the classroom context). They also tend to be input-poor, with an emphasis on making students speak or write from the outset. Nevertheless, many teachers either must use textbooks because of school mandates, or choose to use textbooks because they offer benefits such as easier articulation with other teachers, a structured curriculum, ancillary materials such as audio and video, and photos and readings that are often from the target cultures.

Because TPRS emphasizes learning a small number of high-frequency words and phrases to mastery, selecting vocabulary is at the heart of adapting a textbook for TPRS. How do teachers choose which vocabulary words to focus on during the "Establish Meaning" phase?

- Cognates should *not* be selected as focus structures for the day because they tend to be easy to comprehend. With limited time available, a teacher will not devote time to teaching that *Haus* means 'house' and *Maus* means 'mouse.' Cognates can be acquired by students when they are used in storytelling, discussion, or written input without extra focus.
- High-frequency words and phrases—the ones that are used most frequently in everyday life—should be selected as focus structures. It is easy to find lists of the most frequently used words in a given target language online. Some examples include verb forms for 'to be,' and 'to have,' structures like negation, and nouns having to do with time. A simple Google search for some of the words and phrases from a textbook vocabulary list can be used to see which are used more frequently on the Internet. Words and phrases with more results are more frequent and thus more important to feature in class.
- Low-frequency words and phrases need not be taught as focus structures. In any collection of thematic vocabulary, such as personality traits, there are some that will be used more frequently (like "nice" in English), and others that will be used very rarely (like "stingy" in English.) Students are unlikely to remember these rarely used words long-term, so TPRS teachers will avoid teaching them and testing them when possible.

Textbook chapters commonly introduce specific grammatical structures or paradigms. In adapting a textbook for TPRS, teachers may select target phrases that include correct examples of these grammatical structures. For instance, if a Chinese textbook introduces expressing possession using *de*, one of the target phrases chosen for a TPRS class might be *tā de lǎoshī* 'his teacher.' However, teachers who use TPRS also accept that they will not be able to teach all forms and all rules in each textbook chapter. They will not have time to focus on all of the possessive forms—and a story built on the phrases "my teacher," "your teacher," "his teacher," "our teacher," "their teacher" would be an unnatural and boring story. Instead,

TPRS teachers trust that students will be able to continue building their mental representations of grammatical patterns from input over time. Again, TPRS understands and embraces the piecemeal and gradual nature of language acquisition.

Another way that TPRS embraces the natural language acquisition process is by using a variety of grammatical structures as they would be used naturally in communication. In contrast, textbooks "shelter" grammar: They use only grammatical structures that have already been explicitly taught. A textbook will explicitly teach about the present tense, and then everything in the book will be in the present tense until the past tense is explicitly introduced. However, this is not necessary in real-world language acquisition or in TPRS. A question such as "Who traveled over summer vacation?" will be comprehensible to students if they know the words *travel* and *summer* or *vacation*, and if the context makes it clear that we are not talking about what we typically do. Comprehensibility is not necessarily dependent on whether or not they know that the —ed ending signals pastness. (Conversely, if they know the —ed ending but not *travel*, *summer*, or *vacation*, they will not understand the question.) Thus, even though TPRS teachers may select phrases that provide examples of grammar structures introduced in a textbook, they do not restrict themselves to using only grammatical structures that have already been part of classroom discourse.

Once the key structures for each unit are selected, teachers introduce and use them through TPRS. At the end of the unit, they may circle back to a few textbook activities or play the audio or video materials that come with the textbook. Since the class already knows the most important words, these materials should be largely comprehensible.

Assessment

Assessment is important to let students, parents, and the teacher know how the students are progressing in their ability to use the language. However, because input is the most important use of class time, assessment should not take up too much class time. It is also important to assess students in a way that is consistent with the way the class is conducted. Thus, TPRS assessments have some special features: (1) they often include a focus on comprehension, (2) they often feature stories that have been taught in class, (3) they are often unannounced, because the teacher wants to measure what students have acquired and not how well they studied for a test, and (4) they often measure fluency in some way. Here are some types of assessment that are commonly used in TPRS.

- Unannounced vocabulary quizzes (for example, the teacher reads ten words in the target language, and students write down the translations in their first language);

- Reading and answering questions about the reading;
- Listening and answering questions about the listening;
- Timed free writing: Students write as much as they can in ten minutes, and progress over time is measured by the number of words written;
- Displaying comprehension of a story using any of the activities listed at the end of the Ask a Story step.

Miscellaneous TPRS Skills

In addition to those described earlier, there are other smaller skills or "teaching tips" that experienced teachers of TPRS use. These tips are based on introductory workshops on TPRS given by presenters including Blaine Ray, Susan Gross, and Diana Noonan. Donna Tatum-Johns, a TPRS teacher trainer, has summarized them as they appear here.

- **Say it like you mean it!** Ask every question and make every statement as if it is the most interesting thing you have ever heard in your life.
- **Assess constantly.** Each question is an informal assessment. If students answer you, you know they understand. If they don't, you need to find out exactly what they don't understand.
- **Teach to the eyes.** This means that you should constantly be looking at students. This not only helps to hold students accountable, but it also helps show you when they do not understand. Besides, you are interacting with students, not teaching a curriculum!
- **Insert yourself as a character.** This will allow you to ask your students about you in first-person singular and will give them the opportunity to talk to you in the "you" form.
- **Point and pause.** When we speak too quickly, we often make the language incomprehensible to students. Since the target structures for the day are usually written on the board or displayed on a screen, slow yourself down by pointing to the structures of the day and pausing. This gives students processing time.
- **Repeat student answers.** This is a great way to double the frequency of the new structures in the input you are providing, using very little extra time. Repeat correct answers to show you value student contributions, and repeat incorrect answers with a questioning tone.
- **Add a parallel story or a parallel character.** This allows you to increase the frequency of the daily structures in the input by comparing and contrasting the details of different subplots and/or of different characters.
- **Verify information with your actors.** When you are doing a story and you want to involve your actor more directly, you will simply

turn to him/her to verify if the information you are asking is correct (for instance: "Are you a boy?") Once you have an answer from your actor, you will turn to the class and share the information you just learned. This is also a great way to introduce other verb forms to your students if the language you teach has verb inflections.

- **Listen for their answers.** If students don't answer or give a weak response, ask the question or give the statement again. Use pat phrases like: "That was weak." "You must not have understood." "I will try that again." If you get a good answer, act as if the students "guessed" the right answer, and push to get more details.

- **Coach good acting.** Encourage your student actors to be melodramatic and enthusiastic as they react to the situations in the story. Good acting helps liven up your classroom atmosphere. It also helps everyone believe in the story.

- **Think on your feet.** When you think you are ready, stop scripting your questions/stories! Being spontaneous makes the class more lively and engaged.

- **Exaggerate voice inflection and facial expressions.** This makes your story more interesting and believable, as well as more comprehensible.

- **Use your body and posture to show interest.** Your body communicates a lot about how you feel about your students and the class discussion. Facing or leaning towards the person who is speaking, maintaining eye contact, and nodding your head communicate interest. Crossing your arms or looking at your watch communicates disinterest.

- **Laugh!** Allow your students to entertain you. Relax and enjoy yourself.

- **Ask your students for details.** As you add more details the story will become more and more specific. It is the specificity of the details that will allow you to "go back" in the story and ask questions about previously established information.

- **Make your stories compelling.** Your students can't learn the language if they don't listen. Unexpected and/or exaggerated details and personalization are the keys to making students want to listen. And, of course, some of the tips described earlier contribute to making a story compelling.

- **Use a variety of stories.** The brain craves novelty. In addition to silly stories, try real life stories about your students, current events, language experiences, legends, song-based stories, and so on.

- **Personalize!** TPRS is about interacting with students. By using the interests and talents of our students, our stories automatically are more compelling. It also shows our students that we value and respect them as individuals. Find out as much as you can about your students, and use that information in the stories. Talk about school events and current events according to their interests.

Techniques That Complement TPRS

Many teachers who adhere to the principles of TPRS have branched out into techniques other than story-asking. This broader umbrella of teaching techniques is abbreviated as **TCI** (Teaching with Comprehensible Input). One motivation for using other techniques in addition to storytelling is the ACTFL standards, commonly known as the 5 C's: Communication, Cultures, Connections, Comparisons, and Communities. TPRS is clearly anchored in Communication, which is foundational in the five standards. However, because it is focused on student interests, an all-TPRS classroom may not expose students to much cultural information. Using comprehensible input methods other than storytelling (but still following the principles of TPRS) allows teachers to address Cultures and the other ACTFL standards more explicitly.

Culture-based and content-based units can easily be planned as sources of comprehensible input. **Content-Based Storytelling** is an approach developed by Jan Holter Kittok that uses TPRS's storytelling techniques. Instead of student-generated stories, this approach works with authentic stories from the target cultures as well as nonfiction material such as biography, history, and current events. Authentic stories such as *La llorona (The Weeping Woman)* or *Le Petit Prince (The Little Prince)* can be adapted to the level of the learners. Nonfiction (such as an adapted news story about the latest natural disaster in a country that speaks your target language, or the biography of a famous person like Luis Fonsi) helps address the ACTFL standards of Connections (to other subject areas) and Culture. Students may be able to use world knowledge to boost their comprehension of nonfiction in the target language.

MovieTalk is an increasingly popular technique that was originally developed for English as a Second Language and has now been modified and used widely by teachers of other languages. This technique uses video clips as visual supports for the teacher's comprehensible input. Essentially, the teacher narrates and describes what is happening in the film clip in the target language. Short films, advertisements, movie trailers, and clips from longer movies are good sources of video. For beginning learners, teachers from the TCI community often play the clips without the volume on. The teacher pauses the clip frequently in order to describe what is happening and use the repetitive question techniques (circling) to engage students in the storytelling. After the class has discussed the clip during the frequent pauses, the teacher will play the clip from the beginning with the sound and without pausing. Research on MovieTalk has shown that it rapidly boosts listening comprehension. The teacher's narration uses higher-frequency words and is more comprehensible and more interactive than simply watching the clip as you would any movie. MovieTalk targets the Communication standard but can also address all four of the other standards, depending on the film clip chosen and the goals of the discussion.

Finally, while classical TPRS requires nothing more than a chalkboard, today classrooms are increasingly equipped with technology. There are several online resources that are particularly useful as potential sources of (carefully chosen) authentic comprehensible input. Twitter provides short samples of authentic language from around the world. Many sites offer songs and videos in the target language (including Lyrics Training, which shows some of the song lyrics while asking listeners to fill in blanks, cloze-style). Google image search is quite useful for finding authentic photos that can serve as visual aids for comprehensible input, as well as memes (humorous images with text) containing small amounts of the target language. There are also sites geared towards learners, such as News in Slow Spanish, Zachary Jones, Señor Wooly, LingQ, and Fluency Matters. If the teacher is creating his/her own comprehensible input, other websites allow the creation of comic strips and creation, editing, or subtitling of videos. And simple technologies such as PowerPoint or Prezi can be used to assemble visuals to support comprehensible input.

Current Research on TPRS

Because TPRS was developed by a high school teacher (in contrast to TPR, which was developed by a college professor), research on the method has been rather sparse. Practitioners originally pointed to the body of research on related topics such as comprehensible input, free voluntary reading, mastery learning, and brain-based learning to support TPRS. However, since about 2009, enough empirical research has been conducted on TPRS itself that we have a reasonably accurate picture of how it fares, both on its own and in comparison to other teaching methods.

There have been over twenty studies directly comparing TPRS to other teaching methods. The most common competitor is "traditional" teaching, which is characterized by use of a grammar-based syllabus and textbook, exercises demanding student output and grammatical accuracy, and teaching a large set of (often thematically organized) vocabulary. Other methods that have been compared to TPRS include the audiolingual method, grammar-translation, and communicative language teaching. About 2/3 of the comparative studies find benefits for TPRS with no disadvantages—meaning that TPRS students equal or outperform the students experiencing the other teaching methods on every measure. The last 1/3 of the studies show mixed results, with TPRS students outperforming other students on some measures, and underperforming them on other measures. Breaking down the results of the comparative studies, we find that TPRS shows the clearest advantages for the acquisition of vocabulary and grammar, as well as the development of reading and speaking skills. Additionally, TPRS outperforms other methods on rate of learning; students in TPRS classes get more language and more skill faster than in traditional classes. For instance, eleven studies have specifically tested vocabulary in TPRS students vs. students of other teaching methods. Of these eleven studies, TPRS outperforms other methods in seven, equals other methods in three, and underperforms other methods in only one study.

In addition to the studies comparing TPRS to other methods, there have been more than a dozen studies of TPRS on its own. Findings from most of these studies show that TPRS positively influences attitudes towards class and desire to continue taking language classes. Some also show significant student gains in language performance over the course of a semester or year. For a review of these studies with a complete bibliography, consult my book chapter *Research on TPR Storytelling* in the Suggested Further Readings section.

Quiz

Take the following short quiz to see what you have learned in this section. The answers are provided at the end.

1. Which of these questions would be the easiest for students to answer?

   a. Is Washington, D.C., the capital of Argentina?
   b. What is the capital of Argentina?
   c. Why is Buenos Aires the capital of Argentina?

2. Which is true of explicit grammar teaching in TPRS?

   a. Grammar should never be explicitly taught.
   b. Grammar explanations should be very short.
   c. Grammar explanations should be done in the target language.

3. Which term describes the activity where students read one or more basic versions of a text before reading the full version?

   a. embedded reading
   b. free voluntary reading
   c. authentic reading

4. TPRS does not stress the use of "authentic" texts (texts written by speakers of the target language, for speakers of the target language). Why?

   a. Students are not interested in them.
   b. They typically contain too much unknown vocabulary.
   c. They are too juvenile for adult learners.

5. Which of the ACTFL standards does TPRS primarily focus on?

    a. Communities
    b. Connections
    c. Communication

6. Which is NOT true of TPRS research?

    a. We have more than twenty years of research on the effectiveness of TPRS.
    b. TPRS has shown particular benefits for vocabulary, speaking, and reading.
    c. In studies to date, TPRS students generally equal or outperform non-TPRS students.

[Answers. 1. a; 2. b; 3. a; 4. b; 5. c; 6. a]

Summary and Conclusion

In this module, we have examined TPRS as a way to provide comprehensible input to students. TPRS uses three steps to structure class time: (1) establish meaning, (2) ask a story, and (3) reading. Throughout these three steps, teachers use techniques such as comprehension checks, repetitive questioning, and limiting vocabulary in order to make sure that everything they say is comprehensible to learners. Research on TPRS shows that it is effective in developing both receptive and productive language skills.

TPRS has articulated a well-defined set of principles for choosing class activities that create the conditions under which language acquisition can occur. These principles include maximizing input, keeping language comprehensible, focusing on high-frequency words, learning to mastery, concentrating on specific language forms rather than entire grammatical paradigms, centering class on students and their interests, making class compelling for learners, and developing students' comprehension rather than pushing them to produce language.

Whether you use interactive stories in class or not, the principles of TPRS provide a framework for evaluating activities in terms of whether they supply learners with comprehensible input and build fluency. The structure of TPRS facilitates conducting class in the target language even when working with novice students. Co-creating stories together gives teachers and students a shared context that allows them to interpret, express, and negotiate meaning in the target language from the first day of class.

Discussion Questions and Projects

1. Using YouTube, search for a video showing TPR or TPRS in a language you do not speak. Perform the actions and answer the questions along with the class. Do you find the instruction interesting? Is it too fast, too slow, or just right?

2. Select three verbs in your target language that can be acted out (for instance, walk, sleep, and smile). Write a series of TPR commands using them repeatedly, along with proper nouns, cognates, and words you think your students would already know. (Example: Walk. Walk slowly. Walk to the computer. Walk like Michael Jackson. Sleep. Sleep and walk. Sleep and smile. Sleep like a baby. Smile. Smile a lot. Smile at the teacher.) Then, write a series of questions you could ask students about themselves using these verbs during the Establish Meaning step. (Examples: Do you walk to class? Do you smile in class? Who smiles in class? Do you sleep in class? Do you sleep a lot? What time do you sleep?)

3. Create a TPRS-style reading using three verbs to form a one-paragraph story. When you are done, identify parts of the story that you think would be appropriate places for students to provide details if this story were used as a class story. For instance, "There was a girl *named Ruby*" suggests that the students can provide the character's name.

4. Look up the 100 most frequent words in your target language, including articles and function words. Which of those words would be introduced early on in a textbook? Which would not be taught until later? Look at an early chapter in a textbook. Which high-frequency words are part of the core vocabulary for that chapter? Which words in the chapter are low frequency?

5. Write a simple declarative sentence in your target language, and then circle it using a *yes/no* question, *either/or* question, another *yes/no* question, restate the negative and restate the positive, a *wh*-question, and, finally, restate the original sentence with the new detail. How many different questions are you able to ask? How many times do you get to use particular "structures" in your input to someone else?

6. Select a work of literature or an online article in your target language, and count out the first hundred words. Then, count how many of those words you don't know. Would you be ready to read this text with a class or on your own? Now, take the 100-word text, and create two easier versions of it. Each version should be about 1/4 shorter than the previous version and use simpler language.

7. Choose a short video from YouTube, and watch it with the sound off. Narrate the video to yourself in your target language. Is this an "authentic" video? Would it be appropriate for use with your students? What sources can you use to find video clips that are appropriate for learners?

8. Ask a language teacher what principles they use to decide whether an activity is a good use of class time. Do they mention any of the principles given here? Are their principles compatible with a comprehensible input/TPRS approach to language teaching?

Suggested Further Reading

Asher, J. (2009). *Learning another language through actions* (7th ed.). Los Gatos, CA: Sky Oaks.

Hu, M., & Nation, I.S.P. (2000). Unknown vocabulary density and reading comprehension. *Reading in a Foreign Language, 13*(1): 403–430.

Krashen, S. (1982). *Principles and practice in Second Language Acquisition.* Oxford: Pergamon.

Krashen, S. (1985). *The input hypothesis: Issues and implications.* London: Longman.

Lichtman, K. (2015). Research on TPR storytelling. In B. Ray & C. Seely, *Fluency through TPR storytelling* (7th ed., pp. 364–380). Berkeley: Command Performance Language Institute.

Ray, B. (1990). *Look, I can talk!* (Spanish version). Los Gatos, CA: Sky Oaks.

Ray, B., & Seely, C. (1997). *Fluency through TPR storytelling: Achieving real language acquisition in school* (1st ed.). Berkeley, CA: Command Performance Language Institute.

Ray, B., & Seely, C. (2015). *Fluency through TPR storytelling: Achieving real language acquisition in school* (7th ed.). Berkeley, CA: Command Performance Language Institute.

Van Patten, B. (2017). *While we're on the topic: BVP on language, acquisition, and classroom practice.* Alexandria, VA: American Council on the Teaching of Foreign Languages.

Waltz, T.T. (2015). *TPRS with Chinese characteristics: Making students fluent and literate through comprehensible input.* Squid for Brains. Available at https://squidforbrains.com/